ACCESSORIES

Style Secrets for Girls

STEPHANIE TURNBULL

SAUNDERS
BOOK COMPANY

Published by Saunders Book Company
27 Stewart Road, Collingwood, ON Canada L9Y 4M7

Library of Congress Cataloging-in-Publication Data

Turnbull, Stephanie.
Accessories: Style secrets for girls /
by Stephanie Turnbull
pages cm.—(Girl talk)
Includes index.
Summary: "Students explore the world of accessories as they learn
about fashions from the past and trends for the future. Step-by-step DIY projects include making
necklaces, earrings, bracelets, bows, and scarves. Students will accessorize in style and learn how to make
each accessory work together to form the perfect outfits"—Provided by publisher.
ISBN 978-1-77092-200-6 (paperback)
1. Handicraft for girls—Juvenile literature. 2. Dress accessories—Juvenile literature. I. Title.
TT171.T87 2013
646'.3—dc23
                    2012040043

Created by Appleseed Editions Ltd,
Designed and illustrated by Guy Callaby
Edited by Mary-Jane Wilkins

Picture credits

t = top, b = bottom, l = left, r = right, c = center
title page iStockphoto/Thinkstock; page 2t & b iStockphoto/Thinkstock; 3 iStockphoto/Thinkstock; 4tl Vudhikrai,
tr Karkas/both Shutterstock, Tinkerbell earrings Hemera/Thinkstock, sun earrings Alena Ozerova, hat urfin, bag
Teerasak, belt Karkas, ring Africa Studio, scarf Rustamir, sapphire ring elen studio, br Vanessa Nel/all Shutterstock;
5t Oskin Pavel/Shutterstock, c iStockphoto/Thinkstock; 6 MANDY GODBEHEAR/Shutterstock;
7tl Jupiterimages/Thinkstock, tr Hemera/Thinkstock, bl Shebeko, br Litvin Leonid/both Shutterstock,
c iStockphoto/Thinkstock, bl Melica/Shutterstock, br maxim ibragimov/Shutterstock; 8l bociek666,
r Nattika/both Shutterstock, b Pal Teravagimov/Shutterstock.com; 9 Sandra Cunningham/Shutterstock;
11t Irena Misevic, b ericlefrancais/both Shutterstock; 12tc Megerya Anna, tr Sergey Goruppa,
c Gavran333/all Shutterstock; 13c Guy Callaby, r Malivan_Iuliia/Shutterstock; 14t BananaStock/
Thinkstock, l AISPIX by Image Source/Shutterstock; 16 Darrin Henry/Shutterstock; 17 bl Dmitri
Melnik, br bikeriderlondon/both Shutterstock; 18t George Doyle/Thinkstock, cl iStockphoto/
Thinkstock, cr Tatyana Vychegzhanina/Shutterstock, bl Sparkling Moments Photography/Shutterstock,
bc g215/Shutterstock; 19 tc Margo Harrison, tl Olga Matseyko, c Crystal Kirk, bl pink Sandra van der
Steen, green homydesign, tr ChipPix, cl Everett Collection/all Shutterstock, br kojoku/Shutterstock.
com; 20 bl Sandra van der Steen, br Polyraz/both Shutterstock; 22 flowery bag holbox, pink David
Asch, yellow HadK, blue r Karkas, blue l f9photos, b Monkey Business Images/all Shutterstock;
23t Elif Eren, b Reinhold Leitner/both Shutterstock; 24 bl ultimathule, l Galina Barskaya/both
Shutterstock; 26 tr sommthink, c Vlue, bl cristi 180884/all Shutterstock; 27 Grant Terry/
Shutterstock; 28c Hannamariah, b Ragnarok/both Shutterstock; 29 tl Iakov Filimonov, c ekipaj,
b Blend Images, r Anneka/all Shutterstock; 30 Radu Razvan/Shutterstock; 31 FrameAngel/
Shutterstock; 32 iStockphoto/Thinkstock

Front cover: terekhov igor/Shutterstock

Printed in the United States at Corporate Graphics in North Mankato, Minnesota.

DAD5005
052013
9 8 7 6 5 4 3 2 1

Contents

Accessorize in Style

Accessories are the fabulous extras you wear to create stylish outfits. Think jewelry, scarves, bags, belts, hats. The key is to choose accessories with care and make sure they work well together. Start with these essential rules.

Less Is More

Never wear too many accessories. Pick one main item and don't ruin its impact by adding lots of other things. For example, big earrings look much better if you're not also wearing a chunky necklace, thick bangles and a flower in your hair!

Draw attention to a striking bracelet by teaming it with dainty earrings.

Look in the mirror. Do your accessories improve your outfit? If not, take them off!

Plan Properly

Always choose accessories that go with the color and style of your outfit. A thick, sparkly silver belt or bright, feathery hair clip can liven up a plain, black dress, while a bold, stripy top may just need a thin bracelet or simple headband.

Pssst... Hot Tip!

Look out for these tips throughout the book. They give you all kinds of extra style tips, tricks, and help.

Feel Good

Accessories should help you look good and feel confident, not get in the way or make you uncomfortable. Heavy earrings, tight headbands, or itchy scarves are just not worth the trouble—ditch them and try something else!

If some earrings hurt your ears, try other styles.

stud

clip-on

hoop

dangle

From the 17th to 19th centuries, some women wore a chain belt called a chatelaine. They hung keys, scissors, hankies, and other useful odds and ends on it.

For many years, elegant ladies wore gloves and carried elaborate fans.

Parasols were a must-have for ancient Greek, Roman, and Chinese women.

Smart Thinking

There are many clever ways of creating a huge collection of exciting and unusual accessories without spending a fortune! Read on to find out more.

Clever Shopping

When shopping, choose a few cheaper things that go with lots of clothes instead of one expensive item that you're unlikely to wear much. Always look in thrift stores for interesting bags, belts, and scarves. You never know what you might find.

Pssst... Why not have an accessory-swapping party with your friends to stock up on new stuff and give away things you don't want?

Cheap, tacky jewelry is fun to buy, but try not to wear it all at once!

Inventive Ideas

You might not need to buy new accessories if you make the most of those you already have. A long necklace could be wound round your wrist as a bracelet one day . . .

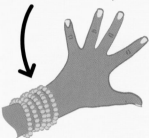

. . . entwined with another the next . . .

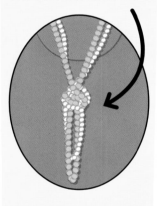

. . . then worn as a belt the day after.

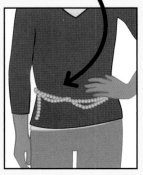

Reuse and Recycle

Making your own accessories is easier than you think, but you need materials. Save bits of ribbon, lace, yarn, and fabric, cut pretty buttons off old clothes, and keep broken jewelry. There may be beads or clasps you can reuse.

Collect regular craft materials, but keep an open mind, too—what about ribbons from chocolate boxes?

Useful Tools

The accessory-making ideas in this book don't need fancy equipment or special skills, but you will need a few basic tools such as a needle and thread, or **fabric glue** if you prefer not to sew. **Pliers** are handy for bending wire into shape.

Brilliant Beads

Beads come in fantastic colors, shapes, and sizes and can be made of many materials—wood, glass, plastic, clay, metal, and more. They're perfect for threading on string, ribbon, or thin elastic to become necklaces and bracelets.

Beading Basics

Before you start stringing beads, plan your design. Beads often look better in an alternating pattern of colors or sizes. Decide which color you want to stand out and don't mix too many styles of beads.

Beautiful Beadwork

The oldest pieces of jewelry ever found are 82,000-year-old beads from Morocco. They were made from sea snail shells.

Women from the East African Maasai tribe are famous for making colorful bead jewelry.

Pearls are extremely precious, expensive beads. They form inside clams called pearl oysters.

Perfect Paper Beads

Making your own paper beads is easy—and they look amazing, too.

1. Draw a long, triangular shape on cardboard—about 1.5 in. (4 cm) wide and 10 in. (25 cm) long. Use this as a template to draw triangles on a sheet of wrapping paper, then cut them out.

2. Roll one triangle around a thin paintbrush, straw, or skewer. Be careful to keep it straight. Cover the last bit with glue so that it sticks down as you roll.

3. Gently slide off the bead and roll another. When all the beads are dry, neaten the ends by snipping across with sharp scissors.

4. Paint the beads with clear nail polish to make them strong and shiny. Prop them up to dry.

5. Thread your beads onto thin elastic. Add small plastic beads, too, if you want.

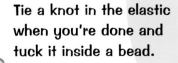

Tie a knot in the elastic when you're done and tuck it inside a bead.

Or glue beads on a piece of cardstock and stick a safety pin on the back to make a brooch.

Pssst... Experiment with different wrapping paper to make a variety of attractive beads.

Fun with Thread

With a bit of imagination and a few basic materials, you can transform colorful lengths of thread into all kinds of eye-catching jewelry without any sewing!

Threaded Shapes

1. *Find a small piece of tissue paper and lay a length of cotton thread on top to make a squiggly pattern. Cover with wide, clear tape and press flat.*

2. *Turn over the paper and do the same thing with another piece of thread.*

3. *Add more layers of thread and tape until the paper is thick, then cut out shapes. Hang them on cord or ribbon as pendants, or tape safety pins to the back to make brooches.*

DIY Earrings

To turn your shapes into earrings, find a pair of unwanted earrings with hooks. Carefully pull the clasp ends apart with pliers to remove them, then make a hole in your paper shape with a needle and push the wire through. Use the pliers to squeeze the ends shut again.

Try attaching several shapes with a needle and thread.

Fabric Scrap Beads

This is a great way of using spare scraps of fabric. **Felt** is perfect as it won't **fray**.

1. Wrap a thin strip of fabric around a plastic drinking straw. Keep it wrapped by winding a long piece of thread around and around then tying the ends together.

Trim the ends of the thread neatly.

2. Cut through the fabric and straw to make a bead. Repeat with the same or different colored fabric and thread to make more beads. String them onto elastic to make necklaces and bracelets.

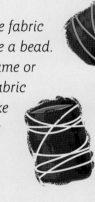

Fluffy Stuff

Try wrapping mini pom-poms in thread, or wind yarn around and around to make multi-colored puffs. To string them onto a necklace or bracelet, thread elastic on a **darning needle**, and carefully push it through each ball.

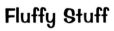

Pssst... Ask an adult to help if you're unsure about using pliers.

Super Sculpting

To create big, bold pendants, beads, and bracelets, you can buy special clay from an arts and crafts shop—but it's cheaper and simpler to make your own modeling dough.

Instant Dough

1. In a large bowl, mix ½ c. (120 mL) flour, ½ c. (120 mL) salt, ⅓ c. (80 mL) warm water and 1 tsp (5 mL) oil.

2. Make the mixture into a ball and **knead** it on a floury surface for a few minutes. Add a few drops of water if it's too dry, or a sprinkle of flour if it's sticky.

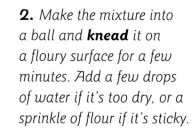

Making Shapes

Once your dough feels smooth and stretchy, roll it out and cut shapes with cookie cutters or mold it with your fingers. Be inventive!

Press textured material on the dough to leave a pattern.

Stick bits together with a dab of water.

Push in a paper clip to make a handy hook or make holes in beads or pendants so you can thread them later.

Bake and Paint

To set your shapes hard, put them on a baking tray in the oven at 350° F (177° C) for about 20 minutes. When they're cool, paint them with **poster paints**. Apply several layers so the color won't crack or fade. When the paint is dry, dab on fine details with a toothpick.

You could also stick on sequins or plastic gems, or finish with a coat of clear nail polish to make your jewelry shine.

Pssst… Too many bright **primary colors** can make jewelry look as if it's for little kids! Mix colors and add white to create subtle, sophisticated shades.

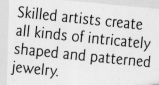

Skilled artists create all kinds of intricately shaped and patterned jewelry.

Neat Knotting

For a different type of bracelet or necklace, don't hide the cord or string. Use it to create patterns that are as stylish as the beads you thread on it! This clever knotting skill is called **macramé**.

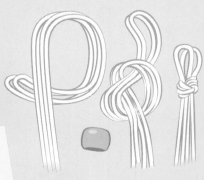

Macramé is used to make braided bands known as friendship bracelets.

String Bracelet

All you need is a ball of string and a few beads for threading.

1. First, cut two lengths of string about 6 ft. (2 m) long. Fold them in half.

2. Tie a small loop in the top like this. It should be about the size of your biggest bead.

3. Spread out the strings on the table and trim the two middle ones to about half the length.

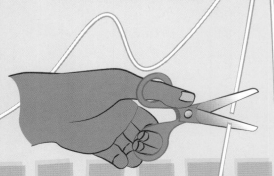

4. *Now tie your first knot by looping the left string over the two middle strings and behind the right string . . .*

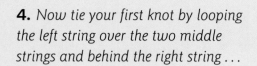

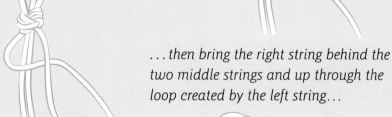

. . . and pull the knot tight. Tug down on the middle strings to stop them from bunching up.

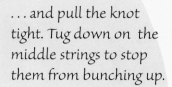

. . . then bring the right string behind the two middle strings and up through the loop created by the left string . . .

5. *Do five more knots in exactly the same way, pulling them tight each time. This creates a neat twist. String a bead on the two middle strings, then do six more knots to make another twist.*

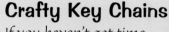

Crafty Key Chains

If you haven't got time to make a bracelet, why not create a dangling knotted key chain instead? Try threading beads on the outer strings to make an interesting pattern, or tie beads on each string at the end of the chain.

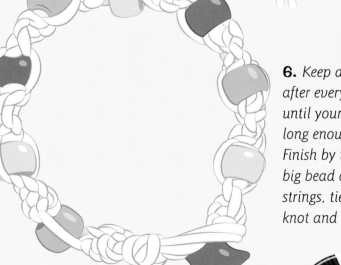

6. *Keep adding beads after every six knots until your bracelet is long enough to wear. Finish by threading a big bead over all four strings, tie them in a knot and trim the ends.*

Push the big bead through the loop to fasten the bracelet.

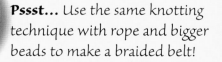

Pssst . . . *Use the same knotting technique with rope and bigger beads to make a braided belt!*

Hair Flair

Hair accessories not only keep your hair neat, they can also complement your outfit perfectly and add a little extra fun or glamour.

Pssst... Wear new hair accessories around the house first to check they'll stay in place all day.

No-Sew Bows

Bows are the perfect hair decoration, whether they're small, girly clips or big, bold scarves. Here are two fuss-free ways of turning ribbons or fabric into stylish hair bows.

Layered Loop Bow

1. *Take a length of ribbon with the same pattern and finish on both sides and make a loop like this.*

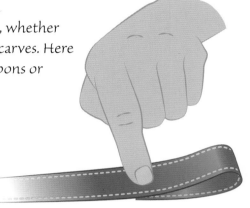

Liven up long hair with several small hair clips or one big, colorful flower or feather.

2. *Make five more loops, each one a little smaller, like this. Cut off any extra ribbon, then tack everything in place with a staple through the middle.*

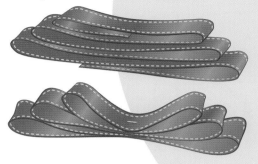

3. *Wrap a short piece of leftover ribbon around the middle and pin it together on the back. Slide a bobby pin through the center and you're ready to wear the bow in your hair!*

For a fancier bow, pin two extra strips of ribbon to the back.

Puffy Bow

This works well with thick ribbon or a silky sash from a dress. There's no cutting involved, so you can unravel it later and use it again.

1. *Fold the material over and over to make a fat roll about 4 in. (10 cm) long. Leave the last bit hanging at the end.*

2. *Wrap an elastic hair tie around the middle of the roll to form a bow.*

3. *Now wrap the end of the material once or twice around the hair tie and tuck it under the tie at the back.*

4. *Gently pull out layers at each side to widen the bow. Poke a headband through the wrapped end at the back.*

For an extra touch of bling, poke a sparkly brooch or earring stud through the middle.

Try making your own hair wreath!

Ancient Roman women often wore hair wreaths made from leaves and flowers.

Women in the late 18th century had huge hairdos that they covered with feathers, flowers, ribbons, pearls, and even ornaments shaped like ships and animals.

Hair Trends

Headbands with springy antennae on top were invented in 1981.

Great Headgear

Hats are the ultimate useful accessory! Thick, knit hats keep your head cozy on cold days, while elegant straw or canvas hats shield you from the hot sun.

Hat fashions don't change fast, so a good hat can last for years.

Love That Hat

There are so many hats in the stores and there's only one way to know which one will look good on you—try them on! Only buy a hat that feels comfortable and goes with several outfits, otherwise it'll just gather dust in the closet.

Think twice before splurging on over-the-top novelty hats!

Personal Touches

A carefully-placed accessory or two can make all the difference to a useful but plain hat. Here are a few ideas to get you started. Remember to choose colors and materials that work with your outfit—and don't make the hat too busy!

Create a stylish band for a straw hat using a scarf, sash or thin belt . . .

. . . or thread beads or shells onto ribbon or cord.

Clip an eye-catching hair accessory or brooch onto a wooly hat, or add a home-made bow (see pages 16–17).

Cut shapes from felt and stick them together with glue or by sewing a button in the middle. Add a safety pin on the back, then clip on your hat.

Decorations like this are called appliqués.

Pssst... Figure out the best spot for a hat accessory by putting on the hat and looking in the mirror.

Hats Through Time

Hats in the early 20th century had huge brims. They were held in place with ribbons or hat pins.

In the 1920s, fitted bell-shaped **cloche** hats were fashionable.

Hat designers still create all kinds of wonderful headgear!

Stylish Scarves

Like hats, scarves are extremely useful. They make handy hair accessories, liven up plain tops and coats, and keep your neck warm! Here are some top tips for making your scarf stand out from the rest.

Get Thinking

Be imaginative with scarves and think of different ways to wear them. A scarf that you normally use to tie a pony tail could become a head band or **bandana**. Long, wide scarves make great shawl-style wraps to wear on the beach or over a party dress.

Beaded Scarves

Scarves and beads go well together. Give a scarf an extra flash of color by threading bright or shiny beads onto the fringed ends, then tying knots to keep the beads in place. Add just a few beads, or make a pattern all the way along.

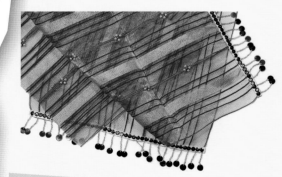

Lightweight, wide scarves are ideal for protecting your head from summer sun.

Study decorated scarves like this to get ideas for your own designs.

Clever Weaving

Here's a fantastic way of adding extra color, texture, and style to a plain knit scarf. All you need is thin ribbon and a darning needle.

1. Cut a piece of ribbon about the same length as your scarf and thread it onto the needle. Carefully weave in and out, along one edge of the scarf. Try to sew in a straight line.

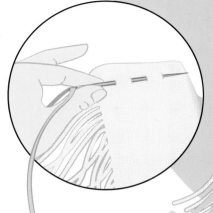

2. Add more lengths of ribbon in the same or different color.

Leave a long end of ribbon like this.

Scrunchy Scarves

Use the same method to add ruffles to a flat, thin neck scarf.

Pssst... Keep thin scarves in place by pinning them with a brooch. For knitted scarves, push the top button of your coat through the yarn.

1. Thread the needle with a long length of thread cord elastic and tie a bead on the end.

2. Starting near the edge at one end, thread the elastic all the way along the scarf, pulling it a little so the scarf scrunches up.

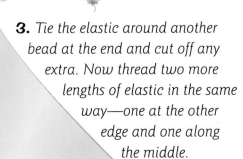

3. Tie the elastic around another bead at the end and cut off any extra. Now thread two more lengths of elastic in the same way—one at the other edge and one along the middle.

Brilliant Bags

Whether you're going to school, on vacation, or to a party, you need a good bag. But don't get carried away. Make sure you have one strong, good-quality bag for everyday use before buying extra ones!

Practical Points

Make sure the bag is big enough for all your stuff. Choose one with pockets, otherwise everything gets jumbled and crushed inside. Long straps that go across your body are good as they leave your hands free.

Clean out your bag regularly so it doesn't get too heavy to carry.

Pssst… Plain cotton **tote bags** are really useful. Personalize them with **fabric pens**!

Denim Pocket Bag

Why not recycle pockets from old pairs of jeans into handbags or purses? It's quick, easy and hardly involves any sewing.

1. Using sharp scissors, cut out a back pocket. Cut up to the **seam** above the pocket to make a flap at the top.

Cut close to seams to prevent fraying. Don't snip any stitching!

2. Braid colorful cord or ribbon to make a strap, or knot a length of string (see pages 14-15). Tie it in a loop.

For a shoulder bag, make sure the strap is long enough.

Bag Decorating

Dress up a plain bag by sewing on buttons and appliqués (see page 19). Add key chains or string charm bracelets or scarves through strap loops.

3. Turn over the pocket and fold back the flap, with the strap underneath. Thread a thick needle and tie a knot at the end. Sew a few stitches down one side of the flap to keep the ends together.

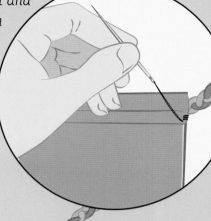

4. Keep sewing across the bag to attach the flap to the pocket. Don't go through to the front of the bag! Go up the other side then tie a knot in the thread and cut it.

5. Decorate your bag by sewing or sticking on buttons, felt shapes, jewels, or sequins. Sew a snap inside to close it.

Handbag Facts

Late 18th-century women carried small drawstring bags called reticules.

The most expensive handbag in the world is a heart-shaped, diamond-studded gold purse that costs more than **$3.8 million.**

Candy wrappers, plastic bottles, tractor tires, and juice boxes have all been turned into bags.

Crafty Skills

Learn to sew, knit, or **crochet** so you can make professional-looking accessories. Why not start with French knitting? It's really simple to do and lets you create all kinds of fantastic knitted designs.

Crochet involves knitting with a hook to form lacy stitches.

Make a Spool

You can buy French knitting **spools**, but it's easy to make your own. Here's how.

1. Find a thick cardboard tube, such as a wrapping paper tube or a poster container (toilet paper tubes are too thin). Cut a section roughly 3 in. (8 cm) long.

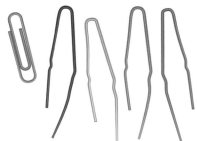

3 in. (8 cm)

2. Take four large paper clips and unfold the ends.

3. Using thick tape, attach the clips firmly around the tube.

4. Carefully bend each clip end outwards slightly with pliers.

Leave about 1 in (2 cm) sticking up.

Knitting Moves

All you need now is a ball of yarn and a darning needle for hooking each stitch.

1. Push the end of the yarn through the spool from top to bottom. Leave about 4 in (10 cm) dangling down. Wind the yarn around one clip.

2. Now wind the yarn around the next clip…

…then around the next two and back to the first.

3. With your left hand, hold the yarn around the back of the first clip above the yarn loop. With your right hand, use the needle to pull the lower loop of yarn up and over the clip.

This traps the loose yarn in place and makes a stitch.

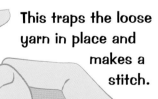

4. Pass the yarn to the next clip and do the same, then the next, and so on. Every so often, tug the end of yarn under the spool to keep the knitting moving through the tube.

5. To finish, cut the yarn, leaving a long end. Take each loop off the clips one by one and thread the cut end of the yarn through them. Pull tight.

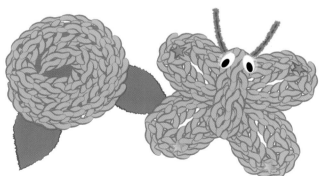

Inventive Ideas

Your cord of knitting could become anything—a flower, a butterfly, a face. Thread the needle on to one end of the yarn to stitch the shape together, then trim any loose ends. Add details with felt and other craft supplies.

Pin or sew your accessories on to clothes, headbands, bags, hats, or scarves.

Pssst… If you're left-handed, hold the loose yarn in your right hand and the needle in your left.

Stands and Storage

Organizing and storing your accessories neatly is vital. Not only does it stop things getting tangled, crushed, or broken, it also helps you find them easily. If you can't see things, you'll never wear them!

Jewelry Boxes

It's a good idea to keep all your jewelry in one place. If you don't have a jewelry box, recycle shiny gift boxes or search thrift stores for delicate glass bowls and other pretty containers.

Stand It Up

A great way of keeping necklaces, bracelets, and rings tidy is to hang them up. You can buy fancy stands, but jewelry shows up best on a plain mug tree. To add a little glamour, give it a coat of gold or silver paint.

Pssst... Save space in jewelry boxes and on stands by removing things you know you'll never wear. Put them in your craft box for recycling.

Handy Hangers

Hang up scarves so you can see them properly. To stop them from wrinkling and make them look more attractive, tie them on bangles first.

Fold each gathered scarf in half and loop it through a bangle . . .

. . . then pull the ends through the loop.

Hang your scarves on door knobs, bed posts, or the ends of curtain rods.

Ask an adult to put up coat hooks for hanging jewelry and scarves.

Earring Display

If you have a large, thin scarf you never wear, why not turn it into an elegant earring holder? It's a great way of keeping earrings paired, and avoids losing tiny earring backs in big jewelry boxes. It also creates an eye-catching display.

1. Remove the glass and back from a picture frame. Lay the frame on the middle of the scarf.

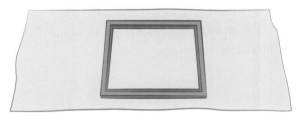

2. Stretch the scarf around the frame. Keep it in place with thumbtacks.

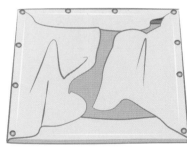

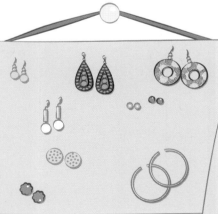

3. Turn it over and hang or pin on earrings. Prop your stand on a dresser or tie ribbon around two of the thumbtacks and hang it up.

Be Inspired

If you want to adapt or create even more accessories, experiment with different materials and methods. Here are a few ways to get your imagination buzzing.

Collect Materials

Visit craft stores, which are packed with accessory-making kits and all kinds of wonderful materials and equipment for making your own designs. Just beware—they may be expensive.

Pssst... Handmade accessories make great gifts for friends and family.

These flowers are made from layers of net and lace.

Try hanging charms on a safety pin in the style of this vintage brooch.

Search for Styles

Top designers often base new looks on classic fashions from the past. Try this by studying ancient jewelry in museums and noting interesting patterns or styles. Look in old photo albums, antique shops, or even your grandma's jewelry box!

Keep Thinking

What about all the other accessories you carry around every day? Could you decorate your cell phone cover, shoelaces, watch strap, purse, or glasses case?

Traditional Indian brides put on dazzling accessories including nose rings, headdresses, and panjas (bracelets attached to rings with chains).

In the past, kings and queens often wore a gold, jewel-encrusted crown that weighed as much as ten potatoes.

Brightly-colored wigs make fun, silly accessories for parties or dress up!

Don't buy boring rain boots, sunglasses, and umbrellas—try something colorful!

Glossary

bandana
A large, usually brightly colored handkerchief worn around the head or neck.

cloche
A bell-shaped hat, popular in the 1920s.

crochet
To create a knitted pattern of yarn or thread using a special hook to loop, wrap, and pull the strands together.

darning needle
A long, thick needle with a large eye (hole).

fabric glue
Special glue for sticking fabrics together. Good quality fabric glue won't wash out.

fabric pens
Special pens with permanent ink that is designed not to fade or wash out of fabric.

felt
Fabric made from matted wool. Felt is easy to cut, cheap to buy, and comes in lots of different colors.

fray
To unravel into loose threads at the edges.

knead
To fold, press, and stretch dough with your hands to work it into a smooth, stretchy lump.

macramé
The art of tying knots to make patterns. As well as bracelets and necklaces, macramé can also be used to create wall hangings, bedspreads, and hammocks.

parasol
A light umbrella used to give shade from the sun.

pliers
A tool with jaws used for gripping small objects and bending wire.

poster paints
Water-based paints in lots of bright colors that are usually sold in bottles, or as powder to mix with water.

primary colors
The three basic colors— red, yellow, and blue— that are combined to make all other colors.

seam
The place where two pieces of fabric have been sewn together.

spool
A cylinder, usually made of wood, plastic, or cardboard.

tote bag
A large bag made of sturdy material, with thick handles and an open top.

Smart Sites

www.save-on-crafts.com/howtomakebows.html
Clear instructions and diagrams for tying all kinds of bows with ribbon.

www.firstpalette.com/Craft_themes/Wearables/Wearables.html
Lots of ideas for wearable crafts, including bracelets, necklaces, bags and much more.

http://vintagefashionguild.org/fashion-history/the-history-of-womens-hats
Fascinating facts about the history of women's hats with photographs.

www.threadbanger.com
Videos by craft enthusiasts showing how to make jewelry and other accessories using recycled materials.

www.free-macrame-patterns.com/macrame-for-kids.html
Clear, step-by-step instructions for macramé bracelets, key rings, bags, belts, and decorations.

http://tlc.howstuffworks.com/family/bead-crafts.htm
A huge range of inventive craft projects using beads.

Index